Duncan the Kookaburra

A real-life rescue

For all animal lovers

.

Once upon a time, a young Kookaburra called Duncan was flying around the bushland with his friends. He was having a lovely day. It was a bright, sunny morning and all the birds were singing. The trees were gently swaying in the breeze. Duncan had not been flying for too long. He was still quite new to this wonderful skill he had learnt from his mum and dad.

On this particular day, he was feeling very brave and adventurous about flying. He was going a little higher and a little further than he had flown before. He swooped up and down and flapped his wings fast, then glided slowly along. He rested on a branch for a bit and then he went off again.

Duncan was having so much fun that he forgot which way he had flown. He could hear loud, strange noises like nothing he had heard before in the bushland. He looked down and saw all these strange coloured, fast-moving objects with little puffs of smoke coming out of the back of them.

Duncan was scared. He didn't like them and so he decided to fly home. He swooped down quickly, but he flew too low. Then, all of a sudden, BANG! A car accidently hit Duncan. He was in the middle of a busy road and was knocked out!

A man stopped his car, got out and picked up Duncan and put him in a bush. He wasn't sure what to do. He was in a hurry to get to work, so he called the Rescuers HQ and asked for help.

"Hi," said the man. "Please help me. There is an injured Kookaburra that has been hit by a car."

"OK, we will get a rescuer there as soon as we can," replied Sue.

Sue called Toni, who was a wildlife rescuer and was very good at helping wild birds that were injured.

"Toni, we have an emergency," said Sue. "A Kookaburra has been hit by a car. He needs help!"

So Toni grabbed her rescue gear, loaded it into her car and set off to find Duncan.

"I hope it's not too late," she thought to herself. "I hope I can find him." She walked around and around the bushland, looking near to every bush, trying to find Duncan.

Then she turned a corner and saw a man on his bike with his little boy. They were standing, staring down at something in the middle of the path. It was Duncan and he was looking rough. He was opening and closing his big mouth to try and frighten them away because he was scared and he couldn't fly anymore. His wing was hanging down at a terrible angle.

"Oh, thank goodness Toni shouted out, here he is."

The man, who was called Jason, and his son, Levi, looked a little confused. "Who are you?" they said.

"I'm Toni, the rescuer," she replied. "I've been looking for an injured Kookaburra and here he is!"

So Toni showed Jason and Levi how she carefully put a towel over Duncan and picked him up very gently and put him into a rescue carrier.

Duncan did not know what was going on. His head hurt, he was dizzy, his wing hurt really badly and he could not move it properly. He tried to puff himself up to scare this strange person and tried to bite her because he thought she might want to hurt him.

Toni carefully placed the carrier into her car and drove to her home where she has a special rescue room. The wildlife room was filled with comfy baskets, cages, heat mats, lamps and food for helping injured or orphaned wildlife.

She gently took Duncan out of the carrier and examined his wing. It looked bad; he needed to see a vet. So Toni called the vets. "Hi. It's Toni," she said. "I have a badly injured Kookaburra. Can I please bring him to you?"

"Of course," said Craig the vet. "You can bring him in now."

So poor Duncan went back in the carrier and in the car to the vets. Toni talked to him on the way. "Don't worry my little pal," she said. "We are going to try and help you." Duncan didn't understand what she said, but her voice was soft and gentle and so he closed his eyes and rested.

Craig the vet looked at Duncan and shook his head. "Oh dear. It doesn't look good," he said. "I think his wing is badly broken."

"Oh no," replied Toni in a sad voice. "Can anything be done to fix it?"

"Well," said Craig, "we will try our best. First he needs an X-ray."

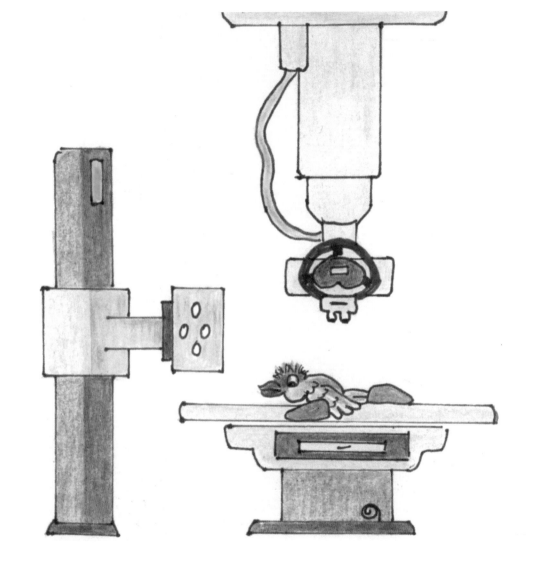

So Duncan was taken into a big room with an enormous machine. He was terrified. They put heavy bags full of sand on his tail and wing tips to keep him still. The machine made a noise and the X-ray was done.

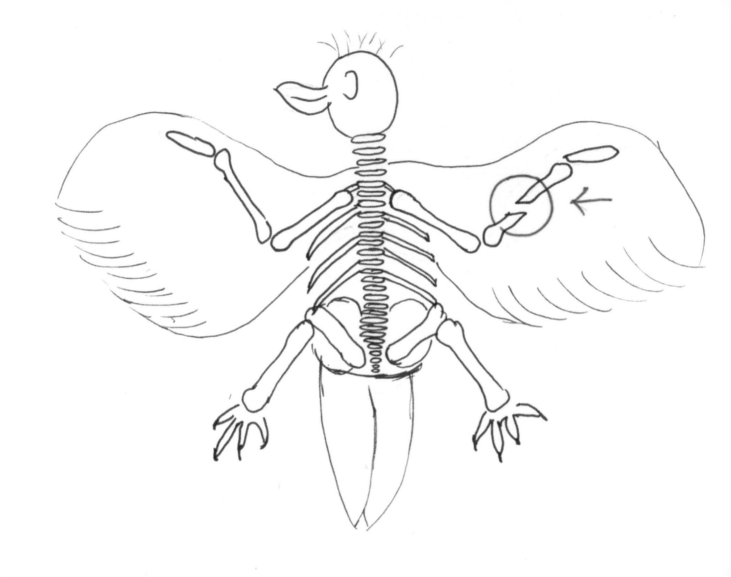

Craig the vet looked at Duncan's X-ray. "It's a bad break I'm afraid," he said to Toni. "I'm not sure we can fix it. Kookaburras need to be able to fly perfectly because they have to hunt for their food. He will need to be able to catch mice for his dinner."

Craig explained that the bones needed to be kept together and very, very still so that they could heal. He took Duncan off to the operating theatre where he moved the bones back together while Duncan was on sleepy gas. He wrapped Duncan's wing in a very big bandage and wrapped it round many, many times.

Toni waited and worried about how it was going. Then Craig came out of the operating room and said, "He's all done. Now, he is not going to understand why he has a bandage and he will try and get it off. I have made it very secure. Our aim is to keep it on for two weeks so his wing bones can heal up."

Duncan was back in the carrier and feeling very sleepy. His wing didn't hurt as much, but it was covered up with strange material and he couldn't move it at all.

Toni got Duncan home to her wildlife rescue room. He was sore, tired and sad; he wanted to go home to the bushland. So when Toni brought him some dinner, he would not eat it.

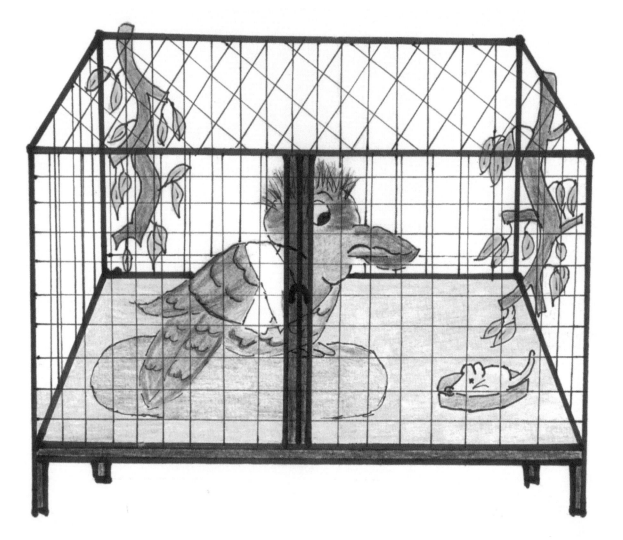

Duncan was in a cage, and it wasn't very big, but this was on purpose to stop him from moving too much and hurting himself. Toni told him in her soft voice, "Hey my little pal, I'm trying to help you and you have to eat. If you don't eat I will have to open your big scary beak and put the food in for you."

Duncan didn't understand. Toni said good night to him and put him on a warm heat pad. She said, "I'll try giving you food again tomorrow."

The next day she brought him a dead mouse to eat, because Kookaburras eat mice in the wild, but Duncan refused to eat it. So Toni gently wrapped him up in the towel, opened his beak and shoved the mouse in. Duncan swallowed. "Phew!" she said. "Now he has some breakfast in his tummy."

Duncan was sad in the tiny cage and didn't eat for five days by himself. Every day, Toni wrapped him up, opened his beak and shoved in his mouse.

On the sixth day, Toni put the dead mouse in Duncan's cage, as usual, and left him alone to see if he would eat. She came back an hour later and Duncan had eaten by himself! "Yay! He must be feeling better," she said.

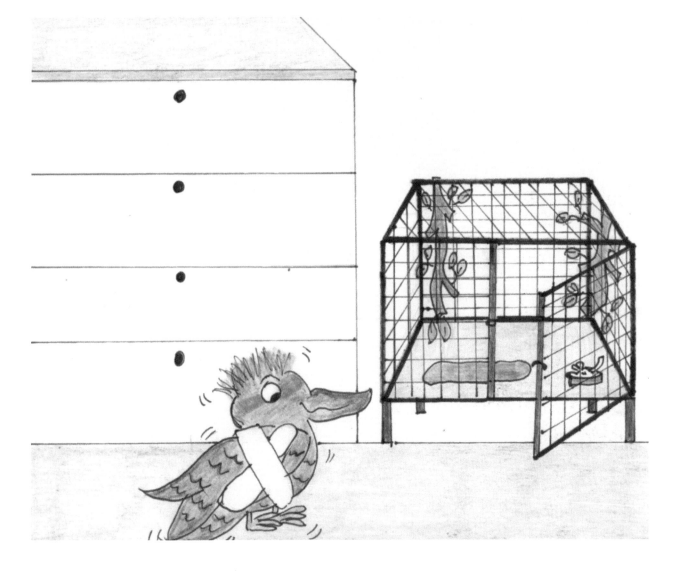

Duncan was feeling better. He wanted to go home. He didn't understand why he was being kept in a cage and he was cross! He bit the cage bars and pushed on them to try and get out.

One day, he pushed on the bars and the cage door flew open. Duncan leapt out and was hopping around on the floor. Toni came in and said, "What is going on? You're a very clever Kookaburra to escape." He was hard to catch; he couldn't fly but he could still run! He ran round and round the room and when Toni tried to catch him he opened his big scary beak at her.

It had been 12 days since Toni had rescued Duncan. He now had a lot of energy and tried to escape every day! He was eating by himself and feeling frustrated in his small cage.

Toni called Craig the vet and said, "I think Duncan has recovered. Can I take off his bandage?"

Yes," said Craig. "It has been 12 days so that's fine to take the bandage off. Let's hope he's healed up well."

Toni knew this was going to be a bit tricky as Duncan just wanted to get back to his bushland. He was cross and didn't understand what was about to happen. She took a deep breath and said, "Right, now please be a good boy. No biting me. I am going to take off your bandage."

Something strange happened that day. Duncan sat still and he was a very well-behaved young Kookaburra. He didn't open his beak once. Toni smiled down at him and said, "Finally you understand that I'm trying to help you! I want to take you back to the bushland and set you free, so you can find your family and be happy. But now we have to make sure you can fly 100% so you can hunt for your food.

Duncan looked at her with his big bright eyes and seemed to understand that this was helping him.

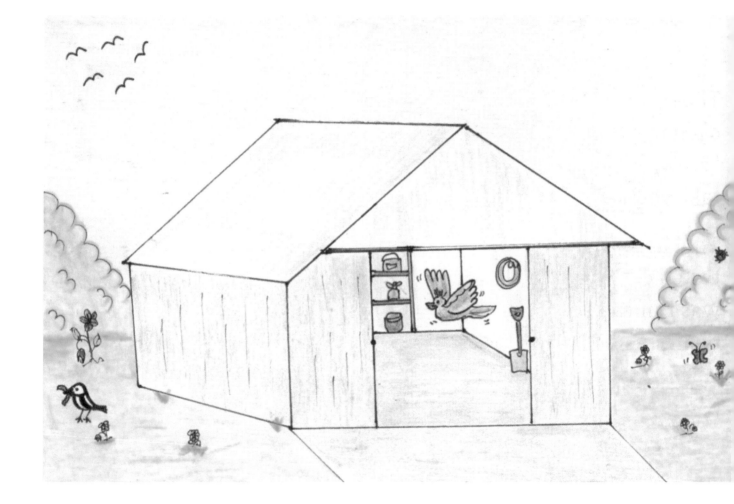

The bandage was off and Duncan's wing was sitting nicely in an even position, just like his other wing. Toni let out a sigh of relief. "Wow, my little pal," she said. "Your wing looks amazing. We can't take you home just yet though. We have to test your flying."

Toni has an enormous shed in her garden where lots of birds have tested out flying before being released back into the wild. Today was Duncan's turn. She carried him out in a towel, shut the door behind them, and let him go. He sat for a moment and then took off. He flew around and around and was very hard to catch again!

"Wow!" said Toni. "You're ready to go home my little friend."

So that evening, Toni called Jason and his son Levi, who had found Duncan, and asked them if they wanted to come and watch Duncan be set free back to his home. They said yes! They would love to come along.

So the next morning, they all met up at the bushland where Duncan came from. Toni also asked Alex, her husband, to come along as everyone loved Duncan very much and wanted to watch him being set free. Toni placed the rescue carrier on the ground near some lovely big trees. Duncan stuck his head out first and then he came out completely. He couldn't believe it! "I'm home," he thought to himself. Just then, he took off, stretched out both his wings beautifully and flew up very high. He circled around and then landed perfectly in a big tree.

Duncan started to call – a very loud call. He was shouting for his family. Kookaburras make a strange call that sounds like monkeys laughing. They sometimes have the nickname of "Laughing Kookaburra".

Just then, the bushland came alive with the sound of many Kookaburras calling, and one flew into the next tree from Duncan. He was home, with his family. Everybody smiled; they were all so happy for Duncan.

Our work is done," said Toni with a smile. She looked up at Duncan and said, "Bye bye my little pal. I'm glad we could fix you."

Duncan looked down and watched her leave the bushland. He did understand and was so glad he had been rescued.

Duncan's Story

Duncan's story is based on his real-life rescue. Here is an actual picture of Duncan and here are some interesting facts about Kookaburras.

Laughing Kookaburras are quite big birds: up to 46cm tall with big strong beaks. They belong to the Kingfisher family and are in fact the biggest bird of the Kingfisher family.

They live in family groups and nest in tree hollows in woodland and forests. They like to live in the same territory all throughout the year. They pair for life. They have between one and four eggs that are incubated for 24 days by the female. Helpers in the family will also help and feed the chicks. They eat insects, frogs, reptiles and mice. They have a loud call that sounds like monkeys laughing.

Dedications

I dedicate this book to my family. To my mum, for showing me care and compassion towards animals when I was a child, and to my dad for supporting this and allowing all the pets! To my sister Heidi, for sharing our special love for animals and for understanding me like no other. I also dedicate this book to my own family; to my daughters Emma and Jena who have been brought up as I was. To Shauna and Max for accepting me as I am. History is repeating itself with their kindness and compassion. To my husband Alex for putting up with sharing his home with my zoo and for his support and help with many animals. I thank all of them for their encouragement in bringing Duncan's story to life. I also thank Duncan, from the bottom of my heart, as seeing him released filled my heart with joy.

Toni Tonge

This book was published thanks to Toni Tonge, Liz Parry, Heidi Thoday and Charles E. Milner

About the author

I have loved animals since I was a young child – any kind of animal. I volunteered as a wildlife carer with a registered wildlife group shortly after moving from the UK to Western Australia. In 2008 I did a Basic Wildlife Rehabilitation Course at the Department of Environment and Conservation in Perth and continued to help animals in my backyard wildlife room.

What gives me the most pleasure is seeing animals in the wild in their own natural habitat, but sometimes our modern world messes this up a bit. So on some occasions, for example being hit by a car, animals need us to step in and help. This is when I help and I love to do this so much. All the stories are based on real-life rescues.

If you ever find an injured animal, try and take it to a vet as soon as possible. Most vets have wildlife carers that help them. They can stay in touch with you and update you on how the animal is doing. All animals need different things. Sometimes the wrong thing can be done by mistake if the animal's needs are not properly understood. It is always best to get help from a vet or wildlife carer.

Printed in Great Britain
by Amazon